Jane Packer's
flowers

photography by **Simon Brown**

text in association with **Jane Martin**

conran
OCTOPUS

First published in 2001 by Conran Octopus Limited
a part of Conran Publishing Group
2–4 Heron Quays
London E14 4JP
www.conran-octopus.co.uk

Commissioning Editor *Bridget Hopkinson*
Editor *Helen Ridge*
Creative Director *Leslie Harrington*
Design *Broadbase*
Production *Alex Wiltshire*

A catalogue record for this book is available from
the British Library

ISBN 1 84091 185 9

Printed and bound in Spain by Bookprint, S.L, Barcelona

contents

The world of flowers has seen a revolution in the twenty-something years since my first experience of the flower industry – working on Saturdays in a local florist. Flowers are much more affordable now, and more widely available, not only from florists but also from street vendors, supermarkets and even petrol stations. The result is that many people now buy flowers on a regular basis, for every day as well as for special occasions.

My aim in this book is to show how to treat flowers simply and naturally. There are no tricks or complicated arrangements, just displays that will appeal to busy people who still want to make a little space in their lives for beautiful things. This book will, I hope, show how even a simple vase of flowers can transform the look or mood of your surroundings, provided that the flowers, the container, the colours and textures are all carefully and imaginatively combined.

Although my formal floristry training was important, so much of what I do with flowers is about having a feel for these different elements; it is really my instinct for what is right that has guided and inspired me over the years. This is what I have tried to share with you here, so that wherever you live or whatever your lifestyle, flowers can be a part of your everyday life. **Jane Packer**

city

Vibrant, clashing colours – scarlets, vermilions, crimsons, shocking pinks, sapphire blues, sherbert oranges, acid yellows and lime greens – capture the spirit of city life. Whether you use them in harmonizing shades of a single colour or in startling, breathtaking combinations, flowers in the city should always look strong and contemporary. You can use flowers to create many moods – elegant, chic, ethnic, exotic, serene or sophisticated – all to enhance their surroundings. Use them to bring out the colours in a nearby painting or to complement a collection of objects. Flowers particularly

suited to city living have strong shapes and definite personalities –
tulips, roses, ranunculus, gerbera, amaryllis and orchids all fit the bill.
Add vegetables and fruit that accentuate the colour and texture of the
flowers to create arrangements that have a bold sense of spontaneity
and an exciting cosmopolitan quality. For containers, use anything
from brilliantly coloured art deco vases to galvanized metal buckets.
If your chosen container isn't waterproof, simply hide a jam jar inside
it. Be as daring, innovative, experimental, quirky or original as you
wish – anything goes in the city.

peppers and gerbera

The vivid, sometimes shocking colours of the city are brought to life in this exuberant display of flowers and vegetables. Glossy yellow peppers surround a red glass vase of hot pink gerbera, bright yellow golden rod and long-stemmed, golden-lemon French tulips, their luscious, clashing colours creating an unusual arrangement. The red wire basket and a few orange snapdragons, their petals speckled with the yellows and pinks of the other flowers, unite the colour scheme.

For a similar display, use whichever fruits or vegetables are in season, but try to keep the top and bottom halves of the arrangement in scale – large-headed flowers may look ungainly combined with small vegetables at the base.

Make sure that the fruit and vegetables you use fit in with the overall scheme, either by choosing colours that harmonize with the flowers or shapes that echo their forms. You might wrap purple-green cabbage leaves around a container of purple delphiniums, for example, or insert glossy green apples into a display of spherical, green silkweed seed heads.

This page: **The furry green calyx of a gerbera.** Left: **This unusual display of yellow peppers with gerbera, golden rod, tulips and snapdragons uses the minimum number of flowers for maximum impact.**

lilies

To me, arum lilies look best on their own with just one or two of their leaves – anything else detracts from their calm, ethereal beauty. The clear glass vase shows off their long, straight stems, which play an important part in the overall effect. Arums are especially suited to spacious rooms in which they make a big impact by standing out from their surroundings. Although expensive, they are long-lasting, and you don't need many for a stunning display.

pumpkins

This striking, textural display is perfect for a modern city interior. Pumpkins and butternut and acorn squash are displayed on a metal platter, which brings out the smooth, steely-blue sheen of the pumpkins. The knobbly blue eucalyptus seed pods highlight the subtle and varied colours of the gourds and complement their irregular skins. Displayed in this way, the pods will dry out and last for several weeks.

green scheme

Delicate, subtle and sophisticated, green flowers are becoming more and more popular, with commercial growers developing new, green varieties of familiar flowers every year.

For this unconventional arrangement, which would suit a smart, urban environment, the various green tones of the flowers – feathery green chrysanthemums, long-stemmed chincherinchees, with their greeny-black domed centres, and the strange-looking, hairy puff-ball seed pods of silkweeds – bring out the mottled greens in the vases.

To fill out the display and to act as contrast with the rounded flower shapes, I added tall, lime green spires of bells of Ireland and sprays of hypericum with their orange-red berries. All the flowers and foliage in the vase will last quite a long time, provided that you add flower-food to the water and change it completely every four or five days.

Other green flowers and foliage that work well together are parrot tulips, zinnias, love-lies-bleeding, guelder roses, hellebores and lady's mantle.

Far left: **A sophisticated scheme of green feathery chrysanthemums, chincherinchees, bells of Ireland, silkweed seed pods and orange hypericum berries.** This page: A silkweed seed pod revealing its soft bristles.

posies

As well as being small, traditional and feminine, posies can also be large, bang up to date and dramatic.

When choosing your flowers for a posy, bear in mind the taste and character of the recipient. Do they like bold, clashing colours or would they prefer the harmonizing tones of a single colour?

The wrappings you choose also have to be carefully considered, as they will affect the posy's mood, emphasizing a flower's colour, shape or personality. There are many different types of paper in various textures and colours, from glossy tissue and crinkly crepe paper to crisp sheets of newspaper. Alternatively, use fabric, such as muslin, hessian, stiff netting or silk. Be inventive when tying your posies, too; choose from silken cord, string, raffia, garden twine, tulle, chiffon or brocade.

Right: **Cream amaryllis, scarlet tulips, crimson roses and laurustinus leaves.** Centre: **Mauve lilac, deep purple hyacinths and lime guelder roses.** Far right: **Green lady's mantle, bright yellow daffodils, fuchsia pink roses and deep coral nerines.**

proteas and dates

Wrapping fabric around a container to highlight either the textures or colours of the flowers is a quick and easy way of uniting an arrangement.

For this display, I wrapped several linen napkins around an earthenware vase and secured them in place with a length of raffia. The colours of the napkins, which were folded so that each colour could be seen, were chosen to bring out the olive green of the dates and the yellows and oranges of the exotic proteas.

I positioned the dates to hang in a bunch over the vase, and made a feature of their heaviness by letting them arrange themselves naturally. I then added the proteas, cutting their stems short so that their heads rested on the rim of the vase.

Neither the dates nor the proteas need any special conditioning. Although proteas are expensive, they are very long-lasting and will even dry naturally in the vase once the water has evaporated.

For a special occasion you could use stately pink and white king proteas in a container wrapped in red velvet or brocade and tied with a silken cord.

hanging tulips

Suspended from the ceiling light fitting with red twine and lilac raffia, these test tubes of lilac and crimson tulips make a light-hearted decoration for any festive occasion. I positioned the tubes over a square glass tank of red amaryllis, variegated pink roses and lilac tulips to continue the glass theme. To link the two elements of the display still further, I criss-crossed the raffia and twine down the barrels of two of the tubes, and twisted red twine around the outside of the tank.

Amaryllis are deservedly popular flowers, especially at Christmas, because their velvety trumpets look marvellous in a wide range of settings. As their stems are long and thick, florists often support them internally with thin sticks or canes, but here I cut the stems short, transforming the flowers from tall, elegant blooms into bursts of vivid colour.

The roses, which look like raspberry-ripple icecream, are a refreshing contrast to the amaryllis. The pale pinks in the roses complement the lilac tulips, while the yellow-fringed petals of the parrot tulips echo the stamens of the amaryllis.

For a fresh, contemporary look, attach the test tubes to the light fitting with shiny or iridescent nylon raffia or twine to catch the light. When making a feature of a few flowers in this way, choose perfect specimens because any faults or flaws will be clearly visible.

bridal bouquet

Wrapped in a long swathe of white tulle, this small bouquet of cream and pale pink roses is sophisticated and understated.

The bouquet is made up of three 'tiers' of roses, with the third tier angled to create a domed effect, and all the stems tied together with soft string or green garden twine at the binding point. Once the bouquet is complete, the string is tied and the stems trimmed level. It should then be placed in water until needed, when it can be wrapped in tulle or whatever your chosen fabric.

Before assembling any bouquet, the flowers need to be conditioned properly; this is particularly important for roses as they're notorious for developing floppy heads. All the thorns and the leaves below binding point should be cut off with a sharp knife, and the bottom 5cm (2in) of stem trimmed. The roses should then be wrapped in newspaper and left to stand in a bucket of cool water and flower-food for at least two hours.

festive garland

The classic festive colour scheme of red and green is given a modern twist with this garland of glaucous green eucalyptus leaves, accompanied by a bowl of rosemary and vermilion chillies, and branches of scarlet holly berries. Eucalyptus and rosemary are both long-lasting and, as their leaves dry out, they will release their fragrance into the air.

I created the garland by fixing stems of eucalyptus to a length of sturdy string with florists' wire. A loop is made in the string at one end, and once the eucalyptus stems have been bound to the string with wire, the other end is looped, so the garland is ready for hanging.

There are many different types of foliage you could use for a garland. If you want it to last for a week or more, there's no point choosing very soft foliage, such as ivy, which will soon wilt, wither or drop. Instead, opt for leaves that will stay the course. Other aromatic foliage includes several varieties of pine, which you can mix for a particular look; blue pine, for example, has a rounded shape while Douglas pine has much longer needles.

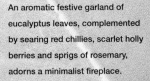

An aromatic festive garland of eucalyptus leaves, complemented by searing red chillies, scarlet holly berries and sprigs of rosemary, adorns a minimalist fireplace.

winter mantelpiece

Using candles, fruit and ivy, the traditional decorations for a mantelpiece decoration, I made a lively winter garland with contemporary appeal. The garland is full of movement as long trails of ivy wind between bunches of grapes, frosted apples and pears and a random selection of gold, silver and cream candles.

The candles are placed in deep glasses, cups and bowls on the mantelpiece to ensure that they won't topple over. Be sure to choose the taller containers carefully as they'll be visible in the finished display. The long ivy stems are then wound around the candles so that they trail over the edge of the mantelpiece, and the fruit is arranged in between. Some of the fruits can be frosted by dabbing on small blobs of white acrylic paint. Once dry, they are burnished with smears of gold or silver acrylic paint.

Dark green ivy and paler green apples, pears and grapes are a welcome injection of colour in this monochrome room. In a green or red room, on the other hand, experiment with ivy, red grapes and green globe artichokes for an opulent effect.

decorative wreaths

These two designs show just how versatile wreaths can be. While the fruit and chilli wreath makes a vivid colour statement and is just right for decorating the front door of a city house, the simple wreath of gold-sprayed branches and roses in test tubes is the perfect wall decoration for a chic party.

The fruit wreath, held on to the door with fuchsia pink raffia, is made with a wire wreath frame covered in sphagnum moss. The red and orange chillies, kumquats and tangerines are attached to the frame with florists' wire. For a less extrovert version, you could try green tulle with green apples and green chillies.

The base of the white rose wreath is made from young, pliable branches such as honeysuckle, forsythia or dogwood, sprayed all over with antique gold paint. Aim for a slightly wild look – the escaping branches give a sense of movement and form a filigree effect. I filled each test tube, with clean water and a single rose, and bound them to the frame with gold wire. Instead of roses you could use a white anemone, gardenia or small camellia.

country

The countryside has always been a great source of inspiration for me, so when I opened my first shop I tried to re-create a little corner of the country in the heart of London. At the time, floristry was still rather traditional and formal, although the whole country look was beginning to infuse it with new life and freedom. My idea of a country-style arrangement is one where the flowers look as if they've just been cut from the garden, even if they have been commercially grown and bought from a florist. I would choose simple, unpretentious flowers with open faces, rather than tight buds, and soft stems, rather than

stiff ones. Marigolds, cornflowers, hollyhocks, cosmos, poppies, sunflowers and some roses all have the right character, and look especially good mixed with other flowers and foliage. Choose greenery that could have been picked from the hedgerow or garden, and include other rural ingredients as well, such as catkins, pine cones, rose hips and fruits. As for the containers, the older and more informal they are the better. Jugs, tea cups and sugar bowls all fit the bill, as do ageing trugs, lichen-covered flowerpots and twig baskets.

cheery daffodils

In the early days of spring, when winter seems reluctant to loosen its grip, one of the best ways to cheer up a room – and yourself – is with a bunch of brightly coloured flowers. Daffodils are among the easiest of flowers to arrange and their radiant colours and wonderful scent make them glorious heralds of spring. Here, they are displayed on their own in a glazed yellow jug, their fresh faces needing no embellishment.

spring colour

Apricot tulips, orange pot marigolds, silkweed flowers and a few nodding catkins are arranged with artless elegance in a rustic jug. Their fresh, sharp colours make them an ideal choice for spring. The chartreuse leaves of the marigolds and silkweeds emulate the green stripes of the tulips and the green centres of the marigolds. Choosing one flower or leaf that brings out the delicate details of another is the sort of colour association I really enjoy making.

afternoon tea

Shape and form play a vital role in this informal arrangement where the star-like clusters of berries contrast with the weeping tendrils of the catkins and the glossy, diamond-shaped ivy leaves. It's not immediately apparent that there are no flowers in this display because the berries and catkins permeate it with colour, life and movement.

The colours of the pretty 1950s' jug echo the colours of the foliage and also suit the informality of the arrangement and the nostalgic tea-time setting.

Cotoneaster, pyracantha, honeysuckle, viburnum and skimmia are among other attractive berried foliage to use in place of the ivy. Florists stock a wide range of ornamental foliage, whatever the season. In summer, you could include an aromatic herb, such as rosemary, lemon balm, parsley, mint or scented geranium leaves.

Sprigs of berried ivy and weeping catkins make a simple but effective display to accompany afternoon tea. This is the sort of arrangement that can be picked from the garden at the last minute, just before your guests arrive.

cool kitchen greens

Many kitchen implements and containers are so attractive that they often have a decorative as well as practical purpose. Draw attention to your old-fashioned tinware or interesting china by filling them with flowers and foliage that accentuate their colour and set off their shape.

For this kitchen arrangement, I used green cottage tulips, white narcissus and cream silkweed flowers. To enhance the informality of the arrangement, I added a few wispy sprigs of foliage: long trails of variegated ivy, to soften the outline of the display, and some sweetly scented tendrils of silvery lavender, which pick up the soft dove-grey of the vase and form a spiky contrast with the smooth, almost sculptural, shape of the tulip flowers and leaves. In the summer, you could combine the same foliage with white, scented pinks, white peonies and the nodding stems of white bleeding hearts.

When combining lots of different ingredients in a display, it's important to have a central theme. For this kitchen arrangement, I've used a colour scheme of green, grey and white.

ranunculus

Ranunculus are the chameleons of the flower world, either delicate and modest or bold and voluptuous. In this display of clashing colours, some of the long curving stems trail lazily over the sides of the 1950s'-style vase, breaking up what would otherwise be a dense mass of flowers and creating a sense of movement. By cutting the stems short, the vivid colours are intensified by concentrating them at one level.

anemones

This mug of scarlet anemones with their mysterious black centres is the simplest evocation of country style. The ideal adornment for an everyday lunch table, it goes perfectly with the red-and-white gingham tablecloth and napkins. It would look equally effective on a windowsill framed by gingham curtains. In this two-colour arrangement of black and red, the only green foliage you can glimpse is the occasional tendril peeking through the clusters of flowers.

dried flowers

Using only one colour and type of flower in containers that co-ordinate with the flowers, such as these dried lavender, roses and hydrangeas in painted terracotta pots, is a modern twist to the traditional country look. Alternatively, you could suspend generous bunches of lavender from varying lengths of chunky rope alongside pots and pans, letting the lavender dry as it hangs.

For the pot display, blocks of flower foam specially formulated for dried flowers are pushed into the containers. The foam for the roses and hydrangeas should stand proud because the finished arrangements have a domed shape. The roses need to be wired singly and the lavender in bunches, but the hydrangea heads can be pushed directly into the foam.

There are many different methods of drying flowers. Freeze-drying is a popular commercial technique which, although more expensive than traditional methods, produces stunning results with the blooms retaining their colour and intensity.

versatile tulips

These two simple, rustic arrangements both use tulips but to very different effect, demonstrating their versatility.

Although there are only parrot tulips in the arrangement on the left, the complex patterns of their pink, yellow and green-streaked petals create plenty of colour and interest. Their fresh green leaves match the apple green of the vase, and the flowers seem to light up their dark surroundings. It's unusual to see tulips cut so short – they look like hot-house blooms treated in this way.

For the display on the right, I chose flowers that would enhance the colours of the rusting table top. The red tulips, streaked with yellow, and the catkins do this perfectly, and the rosy apples draw the eye to its rust-flecked surface. The result is an informal display resulting in an overall relaxed atmosphere.

Left: Intricately patterned parrot tulips, cut very short, resemble exotic hot-house blooms and almost glow against the dark backdrop. Right: A mellow and warming still-life of red and yellow tulips, catkins and apples.

nostalgic flowers

Not every room benefits from a complex flower arrangement, and some country-style rooms look best when decorated with a plain jug of mixed simple flowers or a vase of just one variety. These displays of white ranunculus and lilac in traditional containers are both simple and striking, evoking a romantic rural past.

The elegant serpentine stems of the delicately coloured ranunculus are allowed to fall freely in their galvanized metal churn and arrange themselves naturally. A similar effect could be achieved with marguerites, white China asters, astrantia, even pale pink sweet peas with their curved tendrils.

The scent of lilac is highly evocative of gardens in late spring when its heavy, spicy fragrance fills the air. Sadly, lilac from the garden doesn't last very long in water. The commercially grown variety does fare better but at the expense of its scent, which is lost altogether. Still, in these enamel ewers their impact is undeniable.

Left: **White ranunculus, fringed with pink, in a galvanized metal churn.** Far left: **Sprigs of lilac in rustic enamel ewers.**

soothing still-life

This harmonious arrangement of gently toning flowers matches the aquamarine walls of the hallway. Choosing flowers in varying shades of one pale colour creates a restful effect as the eye is drawn from one vase to the next. The result is a continuous drift of colour, which looks interesting because of the different flowers, tones and textures involved. The flowers I've selected include purple lilac, pale purple snapdragons, pale lilac roses, purple foxgloves, the lower leaves from the foxgloves, and mauve stocks. Together, they release a delicious fragrance – another bonus in the part of the home where first impressions count.

Placing different flower varieties separately in their own vase not only creates a continuous and varied display across the whole shelf, but is also an excellent way of showing off a special collection of containers. You can see that I resisted the temptation of filling every vase – placing a handful of foxglove leaves in one jug or leaving the occasional vase empty adds interest and prevents the arrangement from becoming cluttered.

This page: **Close-up of the exquisite markings of a purple foxglove.**
Right: **Displayed in a collection of aquamarine vases, these majestic summer flowers appear more personal and interesting than if they had been arranged together in a single, large container.**

bedside posy

Fragrant, delicate arrangements are perfect for the intimacy of a country bedroom, and especially for the bedside table where they can be seen up close and their fragrance enjoyed last thing at night and first thing in the morning. White or cream flowers promote a sense of peace and serenity. Here, white peonies and cream stocks contrast beautifully with the dainty bells of lily-of-the-valley. The display is made soft and feminine by cutting the peony stems short and letting them rest on the rim of the vase.

bedside roses

This low arrangement is perfect for a bedside table as it carries a sweet perfume that will linger for many days. The stems of the roses are cut right down and placed in a tiny glass vase as their heads are opening. Delicate blooms such as these need little adornment – a collar of pink-tinged laurustinus buds completes the effect.

sea

You don't have to live by the sea to re-create the wonderfully
serene atmosphere of a cool seashore in your home. The key is
simplicity and harmony – there are no vivid or jarring colours here,
only the pale, soft shades of blues, sea-greens and silver-greys.
For texture, think of rounded shells, sea-smoothed driftwood,
gnarled, salt-encrusted rope and undulating sand. Flowers, while
still a valuable part of the overall scheme, do not dominate or
overwhelm these arrangements. An understated cluster of daisies
or a single white gerbera in the right context have all the qualities

needed for this utterly simple look. And these arrangements can look good regardless of where you live – they are particularly suited to the relaxing atmosphere of the bedroom or the privacy of the bathroom where motifs such as shells or starfish and soft, cool colours often decorate the interior. Among the flowers you can use to re-create this look are silver-blue sea holly, lavender-blue veronica, dried white yarrow, the white and pink flowers of chives which look like sea thrift, pale pink scabious, the silver-blue foliage of lavender, feathery love-in-a-mist and silver-green lamb's ears.

seaside blues

This small still-life of veronica and sea holly immediately suggests the seashore. As I like the ingredients for a sea-style display to look as if they have been gathered on a lazy walk through the sand dunes, I've introduced bottles, pebbles, shells, string and lengths of old rope.

Texture plays an important role: the roughness of the rope and the string binding the bottles together contrasts with the smooth, glassy pebbles and the sheen of the glass bottles. The flowers, too, contrast in texture – the brittle leaves and jagged thistles of the sea holly stand out against the graceful trailing spires of veronica with their soft, feathery leaves.

When choosing flowers for a simple sea-style arrangement like this, you need only a few flower sprigs. Lavish blooms would look out of keeping and disrupt the sense of balance and harmony.

Left: **Seen close up, the delicate spires of veronica resemble underwater seaweed.** Far left: **This arrangement relies for its impact on the choice of contrasting textures in toning cool blues and bleached creamy greys.**

hanging vases

The essence of a cool seashore is captured in these simple hanging glass vases filled with white flowers, pebbles and shells. Suspended from lengths of copper wire, they sway back and forth at the window, as if in a gentle sea breeze, and glint in the sunshine. Colours are pale and harmonious, the pearly, iridescent shells and papery white flowers catching the eye with their purity.

Each vase contains something different, yet their bleached creamy colours and smooth, rounded shapes all harmonize with each other. I placed a few cream pebbles in one vase, then added water to magnify them through the glass, creating a soft-focus quality. Another vase is filled with a collection of pearly shells, including a grey topshell and a small periwinkle. Again, these are placed in water to magnify them and enhance their iridescent qualities. The other two vases are filled with flowers – a single white mophead hydrangea and a few papery white lisianthus, their stems cut very short.

glass flowers

The neutral shades of these unassuming arrangements embody the nostalgic mood of a wintry seashore. Coral pink amaryllis, with their stems cut short, are juxtaposed with seashells in a chunky glass tank. In the other tank, the shoreline is re-created with the starry heads of trachelium, resembling foaming waves, and sea-smoothed pebbles and shells. For this display, a small vase of water is placed inside the tank for the trachelium, and sand trickled between both containers to resemble dunes. I buried one end of the rope in the sand and looped the rest loosely around both the vase and the tank. I then slid shells into the cavity between the two. Arranged in tiers, the trachelium should conceal the necks of both containers.

ethereal orchid

A single, white phalaenopsis orchid in a metal basket filled with stones and driftwood makes a display rich in the silver and white tones of a winter seashore. The translucent and ethereal beauty of the orchid contrasts with the hard, sculptural shapes and textures of the wire basket, stones and driftwood.

To create this display, a galvanized metal container is placed inside the basket, with some stones inserted underneath the basket to bring it up to the right height. Driftwood is then arranged in one corner and Spanish moss draped in and around the basket and weighted down with stones and driftwood, to give the appearance of washed-up fishing nets. The phalaenopsis, still in its flowerpot, is then placed in the metal container, its bamboo support replaced by driftwood. A blanket of stones and driftwood conceals the top of the pot.

seaside still-life

Objects washed up on the shoreline can be transformed into the most compelling still-life displays. In the arrangement featured on the left, a few feathers, accompanied by dried seaweed and a handful of seed pods, take the place of flowers. Arranged artlessly on a kitchen platter resembling driftwood, all the elements combine to create a simple but effective organic display. By sprinkling the contents with scented oil, you could make a stylish alternative to pot-pourri.

Favourite seaside paraphernalia are scattered here and there in the bathroom on the far left. Single, arching stems of veronica are placed in glass bottles, their intense colour picking up the blue of the soap and towels, the cornflower blue dado rail and the amethyst-coloured shells. A starfish and some prized exotic shells line the dado rail, continuing the coastal theme.

Left: **Feathers are used in place of flowers in a simple still-life.** Far left: **Single stems of blue veronica decorate these glass bottles in a seaside-inspired bathroom arrangement.**

This page: **The daisy-like petals of a single white gerbera reflect the shape of the starfish on the shelf.** Right: **Hyacinth flowers remind me of the delicate, waving tentacles of jellyfish, sea urchins and seaweeds.**

hydrangeas

Beach huts and boats are often painted in cerulean blues to match the colours of the sky and sea. I re-created this look by painting the walls in vivid marine blues and tying the pot of blue hydrangeas with turquoise nylon cord. The cord is the same colour as fishermen's nets and, sure enough, some scallop shells have been caught up in it. This style of decoration is ideal for containers on a seaside patio or veranda.

marguerites

Another idea for a veranda is this arrangement of white marguerites in a blue-painted fruit box. The flowerpots are covered over with a layer of sand and pebbles. If you want to put the box on a table, you'll need to line it with thick plastic sheeting first so you can water it without staining the table. Alternatively, you could create the arrangement in an old kitchen sink or drinking trough in the garden.

garden

Easy and relaxed, the flower displays in this chapter are for outdoor living. Even the simplest of arrangements can transform a table setting, enhancing the atmosphere to make family and friends feel even more welcome. There are lavish table decorations for summer weddings, traditional and contemporary table centres for *al fresco* dining, and fun ideas for a children's party. Tight, formal-looking flowers have no part to play here – only large, voluptuous blooms that tumble spontaneously over the sides of their containers. Roses, peonies and delphiniums are popular herbaceous border flowers and are

perfect for outdoor arrangements, as are forget-me-nots, lady's mantle and China asters. But don't forget other garden plants, such as herbs, fruit and vegetables: here, you'll find an unusual display of globe artichokes, but you can also experiment with other produce, such as cabbages and mixed culinary herbs, accentuating their brilliant colours, varying shapes and textures as well as fragrances. And to help create just the right look for a special occasion, make sure you choose your containers with care, from ceramic vases to plastic tumblers, terracotta pots to wirework baskets.

sunny-side up

Daffodils, with their delicate scent and sunny faces, will always raise a smile, no matter how they are displayed. These weathered terracotta pots are the obvious choice for an outdoor arrangement as they blend in with the garden. To achieve the same effect with new pots, all you need do is paint the outside with watered-down natural yogurt and leave them outside for a couple of weeks.

Sunflowers, too, have a sunny disposition. Now available virtually all year round, many varieties last for as long as ten days in water. Always choose stems that have sturdy green leaves covered with down, and reject any with insipid, pale green foliage. If any of the petals turn brown or start to look tatty, pull them out with your fingers. You'll be left with a huge brown or green centre surrounded by a tiny ruff of green leaves, which is particularly striking.

Left: **Daffodils in weathered terracotta flowerpots and galvanized metal containers. Right: A dazzling display of sunflowers and lime green lady's mantle in a glazed earthenware bowl.**

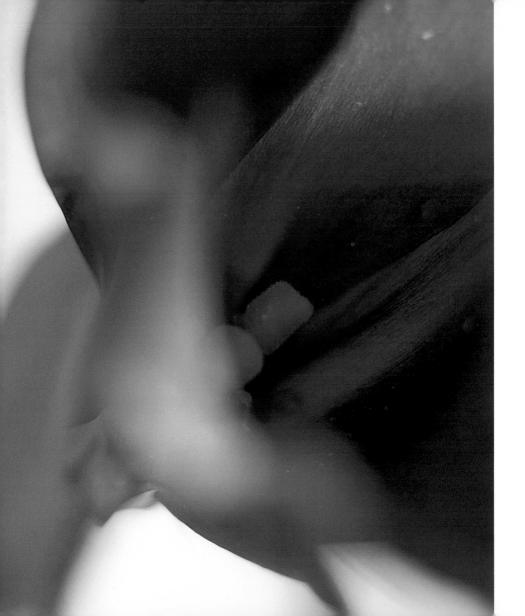

seed-wrapped

Wrapping empty seed packets around a terracotta pot and tying them with raffia is a colourful variation on the idea of wrapping plant leaves around a pot. All too often seed packets are tucked away in drawers or thrown away, but I think their brightly coloured photographs or 1950s'-style illustrations are worth displaying, and provide an easy way of decorating a plain container.

For this fun and quirky arrangement, I chose garish seed packets to set off the rich, purple-velvet lisianthus. By cutting their stems short, the colour of the flowers is accentuated and a simple, compact shape created. The packets are tied to the container with purple raffia. Set against a backdrop of shocking pink tissue paper, it is a riot of clashing colours.

party time

By using bright colours and simple shapes, you're bound to capture a child's imagination. For this children's party arrangement, I chose yellow marigolds, pink China asters and yellow golden rod, all of which can be grown easily from seed. Alternatives might include anemones, ranunculus or gerbera.

These arrangements are so simple, your children can help you to make them. Cut the stems to the same length and place generous handfuls into a selection of multicoloured plastic cups. The cups not only contribute to the bold and happy colour scheme, but also provide a practical alternative to glassware.

You can adapt this idea for an adult party by using little tumblers of flowers to match the glassware, plates and napkins. Lining them up along the centre of the table to create bold splashes of colour or arranging them as place settings makes a novel feature for an informal supper party.

Yellow marigolds, pink China asters and yellow golden rod make up these diminutive arrangements, showing that small is charming as well as beautiful.

garden wedding

For this informal wedding celebration, I used a mix of delphiniums, peonies, Solomon's seal, astilbe and foxgloves – all traditionally grown in mixed herbaceous borders – to complement the style and colour scheme of the garden setting.

The magnificent cherry tree is a focal point in its own right, so in choosing the colour scheme I had to be careful that the flowers weren't overwhelmed by it. I opted for pastel pinks, to harmonize with the tree, and shocking pinks that focus the eye on the table decorations. For vases, I went for shapely ceramic pots in azure blues and greens, which form a dramatic feature yet don't detract from the flowers.

To make the garland, I wrapped handfuls of carpet moss at intervals around a thick, heavy rope with garden twine, and then tied on stems of pink, cerise and white peonies.

Blue delphiniums, pink, white and cerise peonies, Solomon's seal with its bell-shaped flowers, frothy pink astilbe and pale pink foxgloves in bud decorate this informal wedding table. Peonies and carpet moss are used for the rope garland.

peonies

These voluptuous peonies look like old-fashioned roses. With their stems cut short, they make a simple and informal table decoration, perfect for a summer wedding. Leaving a few leaves on the stems ensures that the vivid pinks are not too overwhelming.

bride's posy

This scented and romantic bouquet is based around white peonies, interspersed with pure white roses and the pearl-like flowers of lily-of-the-valley. When choosing flowers for a white or cream bouquet, it can be difficult to match the shades exactly with the bride's dress. To avoid any clashes, choose colours that contrast strongly and deliberately.

candlelit dining

Globe artichoke leaves tied on to a
terracotta flowerpot with two gladioli
leaves makes an unusual candlestick
for an informal supper party. After
securing the leaves, a plastic or metal
container is placed in the pot and the
cavity filled with sphagnum moss.
A large candle is then placed in the
container, together with water and
flower-food. White hydrangeas, cow
parsley and white roses, their stems
cut short, complete the display.

flowers & fruit

You don't need armfuls of flowers to
create an eye-catching table centre.
For this elegant display, a small
bunch of delphiniums, their stems
cut short, and the trailing catkins of
love-lies-bleeding are placed in glass
tumblers in a wirework bowl of plums,
limes, blueberries and grapes that
tumble over the side. A decadent
display of opulence, this arrangement
has a timeless quality and would be
ideal for an outdoor drinks party on
a balmy summer evening.

globe artichokes

The architectural shape of globe artichoke heads, which, strictly speaking, are flower buds, makes them perfect material for contemporary table settings.

This arrangement is very easy to make, although it does involve some forward planning as the flowerpots need painting in advance. I chose Long Tom terracotta pots because their elongated shape complements the bulbous heads of the artichokes. These were painted dark green to match the deepest colour in the artichoke wrapping paper.

For an evening dinner party, hollow out the centre of each artichoke and fill it with a candle or nightlight. For a sophisticated look, gild the artichokes with gold spray paint and paint the pots gold. If artichokes are hard to come by, use green or purple ornamental cabbages instead. If you leave the roots on, they'll last for several weeks.

Globe artichokes in green-painted Long Tom terracotta pots make a striking and contemporary display for an informal outdoor lunch. Sheets of wrapping paper decorated with globe artichokes complement the arrangement perfectly.

acknowledgments

Author's acknowledgments

This title is an abridgement of *Living With Flowers.* The author would like to thank everyone who worked on the original book, especially Simon Brown, who captured everything on film so beautifully; Leslie Harrington, who art directed the book, tirelessly selected the best images and produced such stunning layouts; Jane Struthers for putting everything into the written word so eloquently; Cathy Sinker who searched everywhere for just the right accessories; Jenna Jarman who was responsible for pulling it all into shape; and finally to the team at my shops and school, without whom projects like this would not be possible.

Publisher's acknowledgments

The publisher would like to thank the following for providing locations for photography: Jennifer Alexander; Jackie Altfield at Holt Antique Centre, Holt, Norfolk, 01263 712097; Brocante, Rectory Grove, Leigh-on-Sea, Essex, 01702 470756; Helen Fickling; Nick Grossmark and Graeme Merton; Fianne Stanford at Kirker Greer, Belvedere Road, Burnham-on-Crouch, Essex, 01621 784647; Karen McDonald Thomas, 2, Chapel Yard, Holt, Norfolk, 01263 713935; Christine Stafferton; and Wright and Teague, and Tudor Rose (020 8288 0999) for supplying dried flowers. The publisher would also like to thank Carolyn Harris and Elspeth Alexander for appearing in the book.

Opposite page, from top left, clockwise: **allium, hellebore, widow iris, white ranunclus.**